D0722691

Essentials

ESSENTIALS

JEAN TOOMER

Edited by Rudolph P. Byrd

The University of Georgia Press
Athens and London

Foreword by Rudolph P. Byrd
© 1991 by the University of Georgia Press
Athens, Georgia 30602
Introduction by Gorham B. Munson © 1991 by
Elizabeth Delza Munson
All rights reserved

Jean Toomer's design adapted by Erin Kirk
Set in Bodoni by G & S Typesetters, Inc.
Printed and bound by Thomson-Shore
The paper in this book meets the guidelines for
permanence and durability of the Committee on
Production Guidelines for Book Longevity of the
Council on Library Resources.

Printed in the United States of America

95   94   93   92   91   C   5   4   3   2   1

Library of Congress Cataloging in Publication Data

Toomer, Jean, 1894–1967.
    Essentials / Jean Toomer ; edited by Rudolph P. Byrd.
        p.   cm.
    Originally published: Private ed. Chicago : Printed at the
Lakeside Press, 1931. With new prefatory matter.
    Includes bibliographical references.
    ISBN 0-8203-1333-5 (alk. paper)
    1. Aphorisms and apothegms.   I. Byrd, Rudolph P.   II. Title.
PS3569.0478E85   1991   91-13324
818′.5202—dc20   CIP

British Library Cataloging in Publication Data available

To Keep the Memory of John C. Covington

CONTENTS

ACKNOWLEDGMENTS

The gift of a book can have transforming effects. Such was the case when Michael S. Harper gave me a copy of *Essentials* not long after my first reading of *Cane*. *Essentials* deepened my appreciation of the great leaps of faith and imagination Toomer attempted in *Cane*, and I thank Professor Harper, a true mentor and teacher to so many, for his timely and meaningful gift. Professor Harper also deserves thanks for granting permission to reprint "Kingship" from his *Nightmare Begins Responsibility*.

I wish to thank Patricia Willis, curator in American literature at Yale University's Beinecke Rare Book and Manuscript Library, for her cooperation and permission to proceed with a new edition of *Essentials*.

An unexpected pleasure in my research on *Essentials* was in establishing a correspondence with Mrs. Elizabeth Delza Munson. Gorham B. Munson's introduction is published with Mrs. Munson's permission.

I would be remiss if I failed to acknowledge the support of members of Jean Toomer's family, specifically the late Marjory Content Toomer and Susan Sandberg, both of whom encouraged this undertaking with their advice and hospitality.

I wish to thank Karen Orchard, Executive Editor of the University of Georgia Press, who supported a diffident author through the various stages of review. I also wish to thank Mona Freer, whose editorial suggestions greatly improved this volume.

A special thanks is due Henry A. Leonard for his forbearance; his understanding of *Essentials* runs much deeper than my own.

And many thanks to the Spirit, Who sustains me in all that I do.

FOREWORD

KINGSHIP
Pray: when the soul's
on its knees;
dream: as body runs
upright;
work: when worlds
turn manward;
love: when the image
is not your own.
—Michael S. Harper,
in *Nightmare Begins Responsibility*

When *Essentials* was privately published in Chicago in 1931, Jean Toomer was thirty-seven years old and eight years removed from the artistic and intellectual community in New York City where he was known as the celebrated author of *Cane*.[1] Since 1924, Toomer had been living in Chicago, where he was at the height of his involvement in the psychological system of Georges Ivanovich Gurdjieff, the Russian mystic and psychologist. If we were to cast the various stages of Toomer's long life into the legitimate and useful periods designated by Cynthia E. Kerman and Richard Eldridge in their biography *The Lives of Jean Toomer: A Hunger for Wholeness*, we would, with the appearance of *Essentials*, locate ourselves in the third period in Toomer's life. Kerman and Eldridge aptly term these years "The Gurdjieff Period," from 1924 to 1935, when Toomer was most deeply committed to his work as a lecturer and teacher of Gurdjieff's psychological system.[2]

The other periods in Toomer's eventful life are: the period of his boyhood and young manhood in Washington, D.C., Chicago, and Milwaukee, where he searched for what he termed an "intelligible scheme" under the sometimes disapproving gaze of his grandfather P. B. S. Pinchback; the period of his literary experiments and his emergence as the author of *Cane*; the period of his discovery and advocacy of the theories of Gurdjieff and the search for a superior philosophical and psychological system; the period of his membership and leadership in the Society of Friends; the period of Jungian analysis and intense self-examination that predictably culminated in a return to the teachings of Gurdjieff. All these periods—or "lives" as Kerman and Eldridge also term them—are joined by a single overriding intellectual preoccupation; Toomer's sincere and tireless search for a system of thought that would endow his life with order, purpose, and direction as well as renew his belief in the existence of a transcendent reality.

What distinguishes the Gurdjieff period from the other periods in Toomer's life is that for the first and last time Toomer was not in *search* of an "intelligible scheme"; he believed he had *found* it. "Here was a discipline, an invitation to conscious experiment," wrote Toomer at the threshold of his participation in the Gurdjieff work, "a flexible and complete system, a life and a way to which I felt I could dedicate my whole mind and heart and body and strength."[3] During the years from 1924 to 1935, the growing diffidence and the puzzling lack of direction that marked Toomer's life before and after the publication of *Cane* were replaced by a new sense of order, purposeful activity, and an unwavering belief in the relevance of Gurdjieff's psychological system to the conditions of modern life. Morever, the psychological and spiritual investigations that dominated Toomer's life in the *Cane* years were temporarily suspended during this fruitful and fulfilling period. Generally, it seemed the furies were no longer at his heels, and Toomer enjoyed for a time an inner harmony, optimism, and a kind of certainty regarding the nature and purpose of human existence, the depth of which he had never known and would never know again.

As he assumed important leadership positions among the Quakers of Bucks County, Pennsylvania, Toomer acquired a deepened sense of his own authority and potentiality. But these years of relative stasis and an inner tranquility borne of a deep engagement with meaningful work were brief when compared with the eleven years during which Toomer dedicated himself completely to teaching and promoting Gurdjieff's methods. Even after Toomer's break with Gurdjieff in 1935, a break precipitated by a protracted and unpleasant misunderstanding concerning money that caused Toomer more sorrow than embarrassment, the Washington poet turned again and again to the theories of Gurdjieff.[4]

The psychological system about which Toomer lectured enthusiastically for more than a decade, and of which he was an important representative and highly respected practitioner, is a system of considerable complexity. An amalgamation of Hinduism, Buddhism, and modern psychological theory, three of the most important laws of the Gurdjieff system are that man is a mechanical being, that man lacks unity, and that man lacks consciousness. To overcome this triple oppression and thereby achieve consciousness of which there are four levels, Gurdjieff proposed the practice of what he termed "self-remembering" and "non-identification." The former is an exercise of self-observation, the goal of which is to make one aware of the behavior of one's body; the latter is also an exercise of self-observation, with the goal to break one's identification with one's body. Both exercises, when practiced daily, promised to endow one not only with an awareness of one's fragmented and mechanical behavior but also with consciousness and the potential to experience higher levels of consciousness. Throughout his life and most especially between 1924 to 1935, Toomer was committed totally to Gurdjieff's psychological methods and theories and doubted neither their relevance to modern life nor their applicability to the principal forms of literature.[5]

Toomer's involvement in the Gurdjieff work would have both positive and negative consequences for his own work as an imaginative artist. The positive consequences are that during the Gurdjieff period Toomer was never more committed to the discipline of writing and he was never more productive as a writer. During these years Toomer wrote such novels as "Caromb," "The Gallonwerps," and "Transatlantic"; a collection of short stories entitled "Lost and Dominant"; and such drama as *The Sacred Factory* and "Man's Home Companion." He also completed "The Blue Meridian," his philosophical epic poem of American history and American race relations.[6] Moreover, throughout this period of immense productivity, Toomer turned increasingly to other genres. "Race Problems and Modern Society," his exploration of eugenics as a solution to racial conflict, and "The Hill," his tribute to Alfred Stieglitz, are probably the most provocative of Toomer's essays written and published during this period.[7]

Toomer's experiments with aphorisms produced *Essentials*, a profoundly important work that contains, among many things, Toomer's philosophy of life. Feeling deeply the need to give order and significance to his life during these eventful and fertile years, Toomer became interested in autobiography and began writing "Earth-Being," the earliest of several versions of an autobiography never completed.[8] As Toomer rose to greater eminence in the Gurdjieff hierarchy in the United States and established a large and loyal following in Chicago, he wrote the best and most ambitious works in his rather uneven canon. *Cane*, appearing in 1923, is his most important exception.

Although the Gurdjieff years were Toomer's most prolific as a writer, during this time he wrote very little deserving of publication. Unfortunately, one of the negative consequences of Toomer's immersion in the Gurdjieff work is the disappearance of the lyrical and poetic sensibility that produced *Cane*. With the exception of such works as *The Sacred Factory*, "The Blue Meridian," and *Essentials*, the philosopher-poet of *Cane* all but vanishes. After 1924 we find a spiritual reformer who is at times patronizing and sexist, at other times altruistic and inspirational, but always dogmatic and supremely confident of the beneficial effects of his psychological prescriptions and methods.[9]

As an affirmation of spiritual values in an age of growing materialism, Toomer's fiction, poetry, and drama of this period are worthy of praise, but as literary adaptations of Gurdjieff's rather complex theories on human development they are failures. The theories of Gurdjieff's psychological system are the chief inspiration for Toomer's literary works in the years after *Cane*, and these works, for all the conviction, passion, and imagination that produced them, are little more than propaganda for Gurdjieff's theories of human development.

Moreover, these works, particularly the fiction and drama, are a revealing record of Toomer's idealized image of himself as a catalyst and master teacher, indeed, as the very embodiment of a psychological system he believed was the solution to the growing fragmentation and alienation of his generation.

Needless to say, publishers were far from enthusiastic about what they regarded as Toomer's arcane literary experiments. The uninspiring amalgamation of autobiography, psychological jargon, dogmaticism, and highly contrived plots were not, as many publishers concluded, the promise of a commercial success. The perception that Toomer's new work would interest only an enlightened minority, his predilection for didacticism, and his disregard for the value of verisimilitude would have far-reaching consequences. Most of his works were never published, and this explains, in large part, Toomer's growing obscurity after 1923.

In spite of the negative consequences of Toomer's Gurdjieffian conversion, it is important to remember that not everything Toomer wrote in the years after *Cane* was only propaganda for the Gurdjieff work. Along with *The Sacred Factory* and "The Blue Meridian," *Essentials* is one of the most compelling, unified, and original works of this period. Published privately in 1931 and now made available to a larger audience by the University of Georgia Press, the success and appeal of *Essentials* is due to Toomer's profound understanding of the pathologies, jeopardies, and challenges of life in the modern age and to Toomer's sound judgment in selecting the most efficacious form for his philosophical and psychological meditations.

The literary form Toomer employs throughout *Essentials* is the aphorism. *Essentials* contains several hundred aphorisms and definitions that seem to have crystalized in Toomer in an almost spontaneous fashion from the years 1925 to 1930. In many instances, these fleeting but intense moments of insight are reproduced in *Essentials* in the form in which they first made their imprint upon Toomer's consciousness. As Toomer asserts in the foreword to *Essentials*, with "few exceptions I have left each line as it originally formed." These aphorisms—or "crystallizations," as Toomer also termed them—address a plethora of issues ranging from the dynamics of a spiritual and psychological transformation to the ill effects of the worship of the machine, from the failure of modern religion and education to the limitations of subjective and objective knowledge. As an integrated and coherent collection of philosophical utterances, these "crystallizations" constitute not only the distillation of Gurdjieff's theories but also Toomer's philosophy of life.

While the aphorisms of *Essentials* are the private revelations of an intellectual whose worldview bears the unmistakable imprint of Gurdjieff's theories, they also had a public purpose. Toomer employed many of the aphorisms in *Essentials* as pedagogic aids in his lectures on Gurdjieff's theories of human development. According to Kerman and Eldridge, as a leader of many Gurdjieff study groups in Chicago, Toomer "would write aphorisms . . . on index cards, hand them out, and have members of the groups discuss the significance of the statements."[10] Doubtless, this was an extremely effective technique, one that Toomer learned from the master himself during his four sojourns at Gurdjieff's Institute for the Harmonious Development of Man in Fontaine-bleau, France.[11] As part of his teaching, Gurdjieff displayed his own original aphorisms on the walls of the institute's study house.[12] These aphorisms constituted the most fundamental laws of the Gurdjieff system and as such provided students with a visible framework for the various exercises, discussions, and work assignments that were part of the highly structured environment of the institute.

While many of the aphorisms in *Essentials* were employed in Toomer's teaching, they plainly possess a value independent of their specialized use in the Gurdjieff study groups. The literary value of the aphorisms is discernible in all sixty-four chapters of *Essentials*; indeed, their literary value steadily increases as we proceed line by line, revelation by revelation, to the last finely wrought insight in this slim but dense volume. In each aphorism the elegance of language, the loftiness of thought, and the depth of insight are compelling evidence that in *Essentials* Toomer emerges as an empathic, critical, and oracular intelligence deeply engaged with the most fundamental issues of his and our generations:

> Conscience, the heart of the human world, still beats feebly in our sense of decency.
>
> A symbol is as useful to the spirit as a tool is to the hand.
>
> A running man cannot take a new direction.
>
> Walt Whitman's average man has turned out to be Babbitt.
>
> An artist is he who can balance strong contrasts, who can combine opposing forms and forces in significant unity.

Plainly, the poetic properties of the language, along with its precision, economy, and clarity combine to make *Essentials* nothing less than a superb example of aphoristic writing.

Toomer is not the only American writer to experiment with the aphorism. Although we may find examples of aphoristic writing in the works of the Puritans, Edgar Allan Poe, and Mark Twain, perhaps the most well-known examples of this terse union between poetry and philosophy appear in the journals of Ralph Waldo Emerson and Henry David Thoreau. In an entry dated December 14, 1823, Emerson makes the following observations concerning the various species of beauty: "Material beauty perishes or palls. Intellectual beauty limits admiration to seasons and ages. . . . But moral beauty is lovely, imperishable, perfect. It is dear to the child and to the patriarch, to Heaven, Angel, Man." [13] In two journal entries, the first dated November 3, 1837, and the second April 5, 1838, Thoreau makes the following observations on reflection and nostalgia: "If one would reflect, let him embark on some placid stream, and float with the current"; "This lament for a golden age is only a lament for golden men." [14] Although Toomer never identified the Transcendentalists as models in aphoristic writing (Gurdjieff remains the chief inspiration), these passages exhibit the same preference for economy, rhythm, and beauty that Toomer employed in an effort to give meaning and form to the "crystallizations" of *Essentials*.

The master of aphoristic writing in American literature is Benjamin Franklin. In *The Way to Wealth*, Franklin collected several of the aphorisms of Poor Richard and set them before his readers by adopting the persona of the frugal, prudent, and industrious Father Abraham. Many of the aphorisms in *The Way to Wealth* are not original (as is certainly the case with Toomer's *Essentials*), but are Franklin's refinements of popular sayings that have passed into the collective memory of the nation. The pious musings of Father Abraham are familiar to us all, and some of the most abiding are: "Sloth, like Rust, consumes faster than Labour wears, while the used key is always bright"; "Early to Bed, and early to rise, makes a Man healthy, wealthy and wise"; and "If you would have a faithful Servant, and one that you like, serve yourself." [15]

Whereas Franklin's work exhibits an economy in the manipulation of language along with an appreciation for rhythm, *Essentials* is mercifully free of the admonishments to industry, the glorifications of wealth, and the evident distrust of others that Franklin conceals under the more attractive guises of independence, frugality, and individualism. Although Toomer spent half of his life in Pennsylvania, the state whose major institutions are in many ways a tribute to the foresight and industry of Franklin, it is clear that Toomer, by virtue of his emphasis upon spiritual values, his condemnation of materialism, and his deep faith in the possibilities of humankind, shares more the worldview of the Transcendentalists than that of Franklin. [16]

The writings of Franklin, Emerson, and Thoreau are proof of the existence of a tradition of aphoristic writing in American literature, and Toomer's *Essentials* is a distinguished addition to an old tradition. While *Essentials* is unknown to many readers, this new edition will certainly establish Toomer as an important author of aphorisms of considerable depth and originality. Readers will no doubt conclude that Toomer's *Essentials* is not only equal to the aphoristic writings of Franklin, Emerson, and Thoreau, in the force of its insights and the beauty of its prose, it is also a valiant effort to resuscitate a moribund genre.

Along with its patent literary value, *Essentials* is an important work because it marks the beginning of Toomer's efforts at self-publication. Frustrated by the cold reception of his new "literature . . . of spiritual experience" and angered by the insistence of publishers that he write another *Cane*, Toomer established a press of his own in 1931. With administrative and financial assistance from Yvonne Dupee and her brother Charles, and marketing advice from Gorham B. Munson (all three were admirers of Toomer and practitioners of the Gurdjieff system), Toomer drew up a proposal stating the objectives and policies of this new press:

To encourage, secure, publish and distribute quality literature dealing with all phases of spiritual experience, but particularly with such experiences as they occur in America. By spiritual experience is meant essential experience, experience concerned with and leading to the full balanced growth and development of human beings.

The field is open for a publisher with such an interest. Most of the first-rate publishers have no particular interest in such material, and, if submitted to them, they are likely to reject it. This is because their tastes and their values have been conditioned by 19th century naturalism and rationalism, or by materialism, or by "back to nature and the primitive," exotic, or erotic leanings. They will publish any competent work dealing realistically with things they already know and have experienced.[17]

While this policy statement reflects Toomer's own particular grievances and difficulties as a writer thwarted by what he perceived as the conservative and commercial interests of publishers, the new press was meant to assist not only himself but other writers with similar intellectual interests. Although the only manuscripts approved for publication were the unpublished (and in the opinion of many editors, the unpublishable) manuscripts of Toomer, there was the expectation that this new and unnamed press would become far more than a vanity press.

Designed by Toomer, *Essentials* was printed in 1931 by Lakeside Press of Chicago under the direction of William A. Kittredge. Toomer dedicated *Essentials* to his many friends "in and near" Chicago, friends who had in one form or another supported not only his work in the Gurdjieff system but also this bold, Whitmanesque effort at self-publication. Sadly, Munson's marketing strategies did not produce the desired results. One thousand copies of *Essentials* were printed. Although the book was priced at only $3.00, its sales were disappointingly low. The poverty of readers during the Depression and Toomer's obscurity beyond the circle of intellectuals interested in the Gurdjieff work were important factors in the discouraging sales.

Although *Essentials* was the only offspring born of the publishing collaboration with the Dupees and Munson, this would not be Toomer's last flirtation with self-publication. In 1936 Toomer left Chicago and settled in Doylestown, Pennsylvania, with Marjory Content, his second wife, and together they established the Mill House Experiment, an experimental community modeled after Gurdjieff's institute at Fontainebleau. In an effort to publicize the values and objectives of this experiment in communal living, Toomer published two pamphlets employing the imprint of Mill House, "Living is Developing" (1936) and "Work-Ideas I" (1937). In them Toomer set forth the causes for the fragmentation and alienation in American life, as well as the Gurdjieffian prescriptions that he believed would result in a much-needed reintegration and expansion of consciousness. Like the undertaking in Chicago, the publishing efforts of the Mill House Experiment were far from successful. Both failed to pay for themselves; both failed to create an alternative press for authors of psychological writing; and both failed to establish a reputation for Toomer as the author of a new and dynamic literature of human development.

Along with its pedagogic function, literary value, and its instructive lessons in the perils of self-publication, perhaps the most important aspect of *Essentials* is that it marks a return to the themes and concerns of *Cane*. In *Cane* and *Essentials* Toomer is deeply preoccupied with spirituality, with spiritual health, and with spiritual possibilities. In a much quoted letter to his friend and mentor Waldo Frank, Toomer explains that the "spiritual entity" behind *Cane* "really starts with 'Bona and Paul' (awakening), plunges into 'Kabnis,' emerges in 'Karintha,' swings upward into 'Theatre' and 'Boxseat' and ends (pauses) in 'Harvest Song.'"[18] The "spiritual entity" to which Toomer refers is his most important and recurring theme: modern man's search for wholeness, connection, and resolution in an age of fragmentation, alienation, and exploitation. Toomer would return to the spiritual values of *Cane* in *Essentials;* indeed, his pronouncements in the latter work are the distillation, the very *essentials* of the complex situations of *Cane*. The thematic correspondences between *Cane* and *Essentials* are too numerous to set forth here. Instead, I shall limit my explications to those parts of *Cane* mentioned in Toomer's letter to Frank, those parts of *Cane* that mark the birth and progression of the "spiritual entity" and its reemergence in particular aphorisms from *Essentials*.

In chapter 3 of *Essentials* Toomer writes: "We should have a strong and vivid true sense of ourselves as wholes, made up of both actualities and potentialities. / I would call this last mentioned sense a sense of oneself. Also, I would call it a sense of reality." The point of view expressed in these two aphorisms has profound implications for the situations of Paul Johnson in the story "Bona and Paul," and Ralph Kabnis in the drama *Kabnis*. When Johnson "awakens" to his African ancestry, he discovers new potentialities; he discovers not only beauty in his difference but also the source of his own strength and vitality. Johnson's efforts to pass for white weaken these potentialities, but his acceptance and affirmation of all the strains in his complex ancestry bring him to a new and potent knowledge of himself and of reality. In similar fashion, Kabnis discovers a new potentiality, a "strong vivid true sense" of himself as an African-American when he embraces the history of exploitation and resilience symbolized by the former slave Father John. Plainly, Toomer is suggesting, in both *Cane* and *Essentials*, that the realization of our potentiality, our spiritual growth and development, depends upon the acceptance and affirmation of certain racial and historical realities.

In chapter 29 of *Essentials* Toomer writes: "We are stimulators, not satisfyers." This aphorism is a means of recasting not only the sexual exploitation of the protagonist of "Karintha" but also the protagonists of "Fern" and "Blood-Burning Moon," all of whose stories are told separately in the first section of *Cane*. Karintha, Fernie May Rosen, and Louisa are not perceived as "stimulators," or women with deep intellectual and spiritual potentialities, but as "satisfyers," concubines who exist to fulfill the carnal needs of men. As Toomer suggests in both *Cane* and *Essentials*, this calculated denigration of the humanity and spirituality of women has robbed the nation of much of its genius and strength, and deprived women of a deep, satisfying spiritual life.

"Acceptance of prevailing standards often means we have no standards of our own. / Adjustment to the external world may mean maladjustment to oneself." In these two aphorisms from chapter 12 of *Essentials*, Toomer essentially summarizes the maladies and tragic dimensions of the stories "Theatre" and "Boxseat," which appear in the second section of *Cane*. John's conflicting thoughts of Dorris in "Theatre," and Muriel's weakness in the presence of Dan's strength in "Boxseat," are clearly prefigurements of philosophical positions set forth in *Essentials*. John's complicated rejection of Dorris reveals an absence of confident and independent thinking; John's cowardice is proof that he has no "standards of his own," but only those of his class. Muriel's internal strife and ambivalence toward Dan are an accurate measure of her "maladjustment," that is to say, of her unfortunate adjustment to the standards and values of others.

In chapter 30 of *Essentials* Toomer writes that "communication and communion both are lost arts." Plainly, this aphorism is a return to the poignant condition of the reaper in "Harvest Song," the poem that appears in the second section of *Cane* and precedes "Bona and Paul," the starting point of the "spiritual entity" of *Cane*. The hunger, blindness, thirst, and deafness of the reaper enfeeble his efforts at communication as well as undermine his attempts to establish a meaningful connection with his fellow reapers. This failure at communication and the lack of connection make communion, the fellowship with others born of communication and connection, a desperate indeed vain hope.

Of course, it would be absurd and reductive to assert that *Essentials* is a mere restatement and rewriting of *Cane*, but as the thematic correspondences between these two works clearly illustrate, Toomer's commitment to spiritual values deepened with the passage of time. The philosopher-poet of *Cane* would emerge again with greater force and insight in *Essentials*. The important difference, however, is that as the author of *Cane* Toomer is still in search of that "intelligible scheme" or system of belief in which his yearnings would find fulfillment; as the author of *Essentials* Toomer is free of the doubts of his earlier years. In the teachings of Gurdjieff he discovers a sense of direction, harmony, and order he at times despaired of finding.

But *Essentials* is not only the distillation and further elaboration of the themes and situations of *Cane*; it is finally a testimony of Toomer's most supreme effort to reject the ill-fitting social categories into which his critics and admirers would repeatedly place him. Moreover, *Essentials* is perhaps Toomer's most eloquent attempt to refute the definitions that others would invent to explain him. Like the strange and luminous book that has earned him an honored place in American and African-American liteature, Toomer himself was an amalgamation of disparate but strangely complementary elements. While we are uncertain of *Cane*'s genre, we are certain it is a work of abiding relevance and rare beauty. While we are uncertain of Toomer's racial classification, we are, as we study the aphorisms of *Essentials*, certain of his complex humanity and generous spirit: "I am of no particular race. I am of the human race, a man at large in the human world, preparing a new race" (24). Although history demonstrates that Toomer's efforts to rise above what he regarded as the narrow divisions of race engendered cynicism, suspicion, and condemnation in others, his commitment to spiritual values was sincere, deep, and abiding.[19]

This second edition of *Essentials* is configured in precisely the same manner as the 1931 edition. Toomer's foreword as well as the order and selection of the aphorisms and definitions have not been altered. Gorham Munson wrote a brief introduction to *Essentials* that was never included. In publishing the introduction for the first time, I am motivated by the desire to satisfy the curiosity of readers concerning Munson's opinion of *Essentials* and to call attention to an important collaboration between two major figures in American modernism. Because Munson was one of Toomer's most esteemed colleagues, a practitioner of the Gurdjieff system, and a collaborator in an unsuccessful venture at independent publication, his introduction possesses a certain significance. Although Toomer left no written explanation for his decision to exclude Munson's introduction from the 1931 edition, I suspect Toomer was not entirely pleased with his friend's measured praise and mild endorsements of his first experiment in aphoristic writing. Two years after Toomer's death, in a kind of postscript to his prophetic essay "The Significance of Jean Toomer," which appeared in *Destinations* (1928), Munson wrote that he was not particularly impressed with much of Toomer's writing during the Gurdjieff period and characterized it as "often wooden and embarrassing."[20] While I share Munson's disappointment in the absence of a melic voice in such unpublished novels as "The Gallonwerps" and "Transatlantic," the aphorisms of *Essentials* are very far from "wooden and embarrassing." In his introduction Munson compares *Essentials* to Pascal's *Pensées*; this comparison is an apt and accurate appraisal of Toomer's achievement. Later in his life, Munson clearly underestimated not only the literary value of *Essentials* but also its value as an example of eloquence and craftsmanship for other writers. In *Nightmare Begins Responsibility* (1975), the poet Michael S. Harper would employ *Essentials* as the foundation for his unified and deeply philosophical cluster of poems entitled "Cryptograms."[21]

In 1937 Toomer completed "Remember and Return," a second and unpublished collection of aphorisms that contains many of the aphorisms first published in *Essentials*. It was unnecessary to include selections from "Remember and Return" in this new edition of *Essentials* because a significant number of these later aphorisms are merely a repetition of ideas expressed more forcefully in *Essentials*. Moreover, a representative selection of those aphorisms from "Remember and Return" that constitutes a departure from the concerns first treated in

Essentials are available in Darwin T. Turner's *The Wayward and the Seeking: A Collection of Writings by Jean Toomer* (1980).

Rudolph P. Byrd

NOTES

1. Jean Toomer, born in 1894 in Washington, D.C., died in Doylestown, Pa., in 1967.

2. Cynthia E. Kerman and Richard Eldridge, *The Lives of Jean Toomer: A Hunger for Wholeness* (Baton Rouge: Louisiana State University Press, 1987).

3. Box 66, Folder 8, Jean Toomer Collection, Fisk University Archives, Nashville, Tenn.

4. In chapter 7 of both Nellie Y. McKay's *Jean Toomer, Artist* (Chapel Hill: University of North Carolina Press, 1984) and Kerman and Eldridge's *The Lives of Jean Toomer* one will find a thorough examination of the financial transaction that considerably undermined Toomer's relationship with Gurdjieff.

5. For a clear and straightforward introduction to the major theories of the Gurdjieff system, I recommend P. D. Ouspensky's *The Psychology of Man's Possible Evolution* (1950; rpt. New York: Vintage Books, 1974).

6. With the exception of *The Sacred Factory* and "The Blue Meridian," all the works identified here remain unpublished. Toomer's published and unpublished manuscripts are part of the James Weldon Johnson Memorial Collection of Negro Arts and Letters located in the Beinecke Rare Book and Manuscripts Library, Yale University. Another important repository

of Toomer manuscripts is the Fisk University Special Collections Archives.

7. "Race Problems and Modern Society," in *Man and His World*, ed. Baker Brownell (New York: D. Van Nostrand, 1929); "The Hill," in *America and Alfred Stieglitz: A Collective Portrait*, ed. Waldo Frank et al. (Garden City: New York, 1934).

8. The various versions of Toomer's autobiographies remain unpublished, but excerpts from "Earth-Being" have been published in *The Wayward and the Seeking: A Collection of Writings by Jean Toomer*, ed. Darwin T. Turner (Washington, D.C.: Howard University Press, 1980).

9. The term "spiritual reformer" was created by Darwin T. Turner. See *The Wayward and the Seeking*.

10. Kerman and Eldridge, 176.

11. Toomer visited Gurdjieff's institute for extended periods during the summers of 1924, 1926, 1927, and 1929. Gurdjieff's institute was established in 1922 and dissolved in 1939.

12. Kerman and Eldridge, 189.

13. Tremaine McDowell, ed. *The Romantic Triumph: American Literature from 1830 to 1860* (New York: Macmillan, 1935), 121.

14. Ibid., 255–56.

15. Benjamin Franklin, *The Autobiography and Other Writings* (New York: Viking Penguin, 1986), 215–25.

16. Cotton Mather, "A Christian and His Calling: Two Brief Discourses, 1701," in *An Early American Reader*, ed. J. A. Leo Lemay (Washington, D.C.: United States Information Agency, 1988). Franklin's life's work is in many ways a splendid illustration of the Protestant work ethic propounded by Mather in this essay.

17. Kerman and Eldridge, 191.

18. Toomer to Waldo Frank, 12 December 1922. Box 3, Folder 6, Toomer Collection.

19. Toomer rejected the racial designations "Negro" and "colored" and defined himself as neither "black nor white" but as an American. For an overview of Toomer's racial position see "Reflections on an Earth-Being" in Turner's *The Wayward and the Seeking*. For criticisms of Toomer's racial position see *Memoirs of Waldo Frank*, ed. Alan Trachtenberg (Amherst: University of Massachusetts Press, 1973); Arna Bontemps's "The Negro Renaissance: Jean Toomer and the Harlem Writers of the 1920's" in *Anger and Beyond: The Negro Writer in the United States*, ed. Herbert Hill (New York: Harper and Row, 1966); and Alice Walker's "The Divided Life of Jean Toomer" in *In Search of Our Mothers' Gardens* (New York: Harcourt, Brace and Jovanovich, 1983). If this disagreement over labels proves anything at all, it proves Toomer believed the act of self-definition is a prerogative of the individual and not of society.

20. Kerman and Eldridge, 390.

21. For my discussion of the influence of *Essentials* upon "Cryptograms," in *Nightmare Begins Responsibility* (Urbana: University of Illinois Press, 1975) by Michael S. Harper, see the conclusion of *Jean Toomer's Years With Gurdjieff* (Athens: University of Georgia Press, 1990).

INTRODUCTION

To attempt to form the judgement of a prospective reader is a piece of impertinence from an introducer. Criticism is not his office, and no self-respecting reader wants it from him. I may, however, offer, out of my knowledge of Jean Toomer gained from a long friendship of immense benefit to myself, some advice as how best to approach his volume, *Essentials*.

Obviously, *Essentials* is a trial at direct communication. Ordinarily, a writer or speaker has to use art to communicate anything; that is, he has to persuade or enchant his audience before it will consent to receive his kernel of meaning. But occasionally questions occur to all of us that are really serious and about which we are really in earnest. At such times we turn to some friend and ask real questions, wanting the best and most serious answers he can give. He doesn't have to persuade us to listen, for we are in fact demanding of him to say exactly what at the very back of his mind he really thinks about the problem. He then can be simple and direct, because we are simple and direct.

It is in a mood like this that we should consider the replies to questions about the meaning of life that Mr.

Toomer here presents. There will be those who, baffled by the unusual character of some of his statements, will wonder, not about them, but about the possible source of them. Plato? Buddhist philosophy? Nietzsche, and so on? This will be a mistake and a distraction. Jean Toomer, it is evident from the definiteness of his style, stands very much on his own legs. He is giving, to the best of his ability, the essential data of his own experience as a human being who is trying to grow past the point where Nature ceases to have any interest in us.

A good portion of the prose in *Essentials* is the setting down of ponderings. It will be worth while for the reader to distinguish the difference between meditation, reflection, and pondering. The last is nowadays not much in evidence in American writing. It used to be; there are examples in Poe's miscellaneous notes, in Thoreau's journals. Russian writers are rather given to jotting down their ponderings, usually highly emotionalized. And the classic examples of pondering are in Pascal's *Pensées*. From a purely literary point of view I am glad that Mr. Toomer is reviving the form among us, for surely American writers cannot be content with the present paucity of literary forms in use. How valuable these ponderings are—as well as what the value is of the rhapsodic passages, the poems, the short essays—is not, as I have said, for me to estimate here, though the fact that I am glad to introduce them to the reader attests to my high opinion.

All I shall say is, thoughts can be weighed with far

greater exactitude than most people think, and I recommend the formal weighing of Mr. Toomer's thoughts. Test them for clarity, scope, applicability, illumination, completeness and the other qualities that determine how solid, how heavy, a thought is. Put them on the scales with maxims or proverbs you have thought well of, with aphorisms by Schnitzler, epigrams by La Rochefoucauld, reflections by Coleridge, and so on. In this way you will discover the place (high, low or middling?) of Jean Toomer as a maker of definitions and aphorisms, and this will give pleasure to your sense of literary values. But more than that, you will have forced yourself to concentrate on Mr. Toomer's texts. He is, you will see, a concentrated writer, attaching definite meanings to many words the mind ordinarily slips over. For example, words like "being," "doing," "knowing," "essence" have evidently a strong meaning for him. He demands, it is clear, a concentrated reader. If you are willing to be such, I think you will discover much of deep interest in *Essentials*.

Perhaps you will be convinced by him that "all our lives we have been waiting to live" and will see the futility of this passive attitude. Jean Toomer bases everything on an active attitude towards experience.

Gorham B. Munson

ESSENTIALS

DEFINITIONS

AND

APHORISMS

To my friends in and near Chicago

FOREWORD

This volume is a collection of definitions and sayings bearing on the nature and forms of human existence—some three hundred crystallizations in words of observations and understandings which have arisen in me during a five year period.

For me, the lines contain the gist or heart of the matter; and this is why I call them Essentials. Not the full heart, to be sure; but, I hope, something of it.

With few exceptions I have left each line as it originally formed. I have added no fillers. I have, however, attempted to organize the book so that in addition to having independent meanings the lines might have some measure of meaning in relation to each other.

The totality conveys accurately though not completely my world-view. To this extent it can be said to express my philosophy of life.

J. T.

I

Man is a being potentially able to act with reason according to value.

Values and meanings, though intangible, are held by everyone consciously or unconsciously as the most real and the most important.

The moral functions are efforts towards the realization of true ideas and true aims.

These are my first values: Understanding, Conscience, and Ability.

Conscience, the heart of the human world, still beats feebly in our sense of decency.

II

"Essence-shame is man's lever on himself."

Shame of a weakness implies the presence of a strength.

He who feels ashamed of slavery can win freedom.

He who feels ashamed of ignorance can attain knowledge.

He who feels ashamed of nothingness can be.

III

We should have a strong and vivid true sense of
actuality. We should have a strong and vivid true
sense of potentiality.

We should have a strong and vivid true sense of
ourselves as wholes, made up of both actualities
and potentialities.

I would call this last mentioned sense a sense of
oneself. Also, I would call it a sense of reality.

Modern man is losing his sense of potentiality as
regards himself. Hence he is losing his sense of
himself and of reality.

We are lopsidedly concerned with actualities.

IV

The desire to be has become the desire to belong.

We can belong to things, not to ourselves.

The open conspiracy: "Let's do outside things; inside things are too difficult."

I am not being; I am the obstacles to being.

I am responsible for my own realization.

V

Our aim is to spiritualize the actual and to actualize the potential.

A symbol is as useful to the spirit as a tool is to the hand.

We have many reformers, few transformers.

A man's worth can be measured in terms of his ability to evoke in the essence of a male the wish to be man, to evoke in the essence of a female the wish to be woman.

It is often necessary to intensify one's weaknesses, and the will to overcome them, both at the same time.

VI

We must not expect one act of liberation, one note
of transformation, to produce a whole new being.

It takes a well-spent lifetime, and perhaps more,
to crystallize in us that for which we exist.

The growth of a human being is a dynamic
symphony of forces playing in this field of force
that is ourselves.

We start with gifts. Merit comes from what we
make of them.

All beings find it difficult to merit growth beyond
growth.

VII

Man must add to Nature. Effort is that which
is added.

The aim is not to measure effort but to make it.

Most of our consciousness is based on and arises
from idea. We must have consciousness based on
and arising from effort and from realization.

Realizations are kinds of experience in which
reason, feeling, and sense blend with intensity
and crystallize. They contact reality, and give rise
to new understandings, new feelings, and new
abilities.

Beings develop normally in proportion as they
realize true aims.

VIII

Productivity is my first aim.

I struggle that I may not die through life.

He is soil no longer fertile for me to plant in.

We must husk off even friends—to make way for new friends.

Growing is a stern taking and eliminating, as relentless as life itself.

IX

Let your doing be an exercise, not an exhibition.

Meet life's terms but never accept them.

Do now what you won't be doing an hour
from now.

Reject compromises which give you nothing
because they give you less than you want.

Those who seek peace too often find comfort.

X

Abnormality arises from the wish to have something for nothing, to exist without effort.

Men are inclined either to work without hope, or to hope without work.

We apply to machines what we do not apply to ourselves.

Social ills are caused by man's wish to have results greater than his efforts.

If society, after conditioning people, gave each person what he wished, mankind would be lost.

XI

Man wishes, not the thing, but the appearance of
the thing.

Wishes have no necessary relation to right
functioning, but often are bent on just the reverse.

All our so-called functions are "showy," and we
are exhibitionists in a more profound sense than
ordinary psychology dreams of.

What most people mean by self-development is
that which will make them appear as they wish to
appear.

Man adjusts to what he should not; he is unable to
adjust to what he should.

XII

Acceptance of prevailing standards often means we have no standards of our own.

Adjustment to the external world may mean maladjustment to oneself.

I think there is no evil in the human world save that which causes—to our modes of perception—the essential to be transient, the non-essential to be lasting.

This reversal, which occurs in many forms, is unholy, and the cause of most perversions.

We must know a force greater than our weaknesses.

XIII

We want to be free from the things we want.

Most of us feel we must be mentally fortified in advance of experience. This is one of the reasons why we are buffers rather than experiencers.

Life moves, things happen, when people care.

When people do not care, nothing can happen. There can be only events of inertia.

Caring alone produces events of force.

XIV

We all have a certain "weight," a constant, which we must attach to something.

If we do not attach it, or, rather, if it does not attach itself to ideals, it attaches itself to non-ideals.

If not to illusion then to disillusion.

If not to what is valuable then to what is worthless; if not to essentials then to non-essentials.

This weight must attach itself to something.

XV

We dislike criticisms of our weaknesses; for, when our weaknesses are touched we feel defenseless, helpless.

We hate to feel helpless.

We do not mind the weakness, as such, nor the criticism of it.

We object to the helpless feeling caused by such criticism.

In losing a false base we seem to lose all.

XVI

Fear is a noose that binds until it strangles.

We frequently have our hands tied in regard to
what we really want. This is because often there is
a denial opposed to the affirmation. We are unable
to reconcile them.

The denial is often in the form of fear. We tend to
take the line of least fear. We do not tend to take
the line of greatest positive desire.

We fear to sacrifice lesser to greater values.

All our lives we have been waiting to live.

XVII

We do everything to forfeit, nothing to experience,
what we really want.

Men are most active when evading real issues,
most powerful when rejecting real values.

We love to sacrifice greater to lesser values.

Tell me the person's strongest resistance and I will
tell you what he most wants.

As for what you usually do—everything save
yourself demands it.

XVIII

Everyone has at least an interest in finding an interest.

We are tired of not being intense.

 Some people can endure so little so well that they appear to be satisfied.

Failing to achieve intangible satisfactions, we are compelled to accept tangible dissatisfactions.

Everyone secretly expects and looks forward to the coming of some great event which will gloriously upset him.

XIX

We shuttle back and forth between accepting
the fact that nothing happens and rejecting this
same fact.

With unwilling resignation we accept nothing
happening; then, with an outburst of resolution,
we try to make something happen.

Now and again something does happen.

Success often means increase of the illusion that
we can make things happen.

Failure gives rise to disillusion, but it does not give
freedom.

XX

Men try to run life according to their wishes; life runs itself according to necessity.

Stubbornness of inclination is often mistaken for free strength.

We no longer talk about theories; we talk about human functions. Yes, but we still talk about them.

Whose energy is released when a spring unwinds?

Man is a nerve of the cosmos, dislocated, trying to quiver into place.

XXI

It is well to remember that the Past, though having meaning, cannot serve as an objective for contemporary man.

Each day, and all that it contains, must be a building in the present for the Present and for the Future.

This is no place for him who wants to make his past life better.

I also am an ancestor, a source, an initiator.

True initiative is a self-activating force which needs no sanction save that of awakened conscience.

XXII

A true individual belongs, on the one hand, to no less than himself; and, on the other, to no less than mankind and the entire human world.

He is not conformative but formative.

Individuals are able to create forms; they are force—in contradistinction to the inertia of the mass.

The emergent type of man is neither an emotional type nor an intellectual type; it is both in one, that is, a psychological type, capable of insight into and understanding of the human spirit or psyche.

This is a psychological adventurer: one who, having had the stock experiences of mankind, sets out at right angles to all previous experience to discover new states of being.

XXIII

I am told, "That has been done before." I answer, "Whatever I do has never been done before."

I am told, "That is not done. People do not think and feel and act like that." I answer, "Whatever I do is done."

It is your business into which pocket of your mind your limitations place a notion of me.

Two asses do not make an owl.

Deviltry is delightful but not satisfying. Saintliness is satisfying but not delightful.

XXIV

I am of no particular race. I am of the human
race, a man at large in the human world,
preparing a new race.

I am of no specific region. I am of earth.

I am of no particular class. I am of the human
class, preparing a new class.

I am neither male nor female nor in-between. I am
of sex, with male differentiations.

I am of no special field. I am of the field of being.

XXV

In being I am equal. In being, I know only pure
equality with other beings. In development I am
either equal or inferior or superior.

I have an aim in life, which is: to function, to be
able to function, rather than to misfunction or to
appear to function.

It is as if I have seen the end of the things others
pursue blindly.

The only man who can leave the earth to other
men is he who has won himself.

With an appetite, a hunger for the whole earth, I
can do no more than drink one glass of water and
breathe two lungs of air.

XXVI

I is a word, but the worm is real.

Who is superior among worms?

Men are starved in one half, spoiled in the other.

When one is developing, his acquired traits and values tend to diminish and disappear; while his essential traits and values tend to appear and grow forceful.

A genuine leader is a standard of excellence, having in himself a natural individual centre of functioning.

XXVII

We can be either lonely or Alone.

At the call to be eagles we cling to the ground like fence-posts.

People either feel they can fly or fear they will stumble. Rarely do we sense our ability to walk firm on earth.

We do not possess imagination enough to sense what we are missing.

Let us venerate him who has had the earth's high experiences.

XXVIII

We experience alternating phases of expanded and contracted consciousness, of increased and diminished being.

Depression is caused when we pass from a greater to a lesser state.

In the lesser state we experience the hell of absence.

Happiness is caused when we pass from a lesser to a greater state.

In the greater state we experience the heaven of presence.

XXIX

Each being should bring to the other pure
crystallizations of becoming experience.

Human atmosphere is formed of the blood of the
spirit.

Human relationships are matters of skill and art.
We tend to treat them as matters of convention,
or worse.

We are stimulators, not satisfyers.

Whatever stands between you and that person
stands between you and yourself.

XXX

Communication and communion both are lost arts.

Inferiority is one of our most prevalent feelings; respect one of our rarest.

This is a rare experience: to receive genuine consideration from a fellow being.

We make for ourselves fruitless unnecessary difficulties and then spend our lives overcoming or succumbing to them.

If sex is right, man, no matter how otherwise conditioned, gives some evidence of the great source from whence he came.

XXXI

Because of unbecoming human relationships the
world stinks like an outhouse.

There is no love, no faith, no trust, but what the
world calls forth to violate.

These are not dead; these are among the hopeless
living things.

Far from loving all that breathes we do not love
even those we do love.

Occidental romance has led to Freud.

XXXII

Instead of wishing to be with people, to work and grow with them, we wish to use them. This is one reason why we hate each other.

We have two emblems, namely, the machinegun and the contraceptive.

Most shots are thoughtlessly aimed at an entire person; hence, in attempting to eliminate a bad feature we often kill an otherwise good man.

If two contenders die, who profits?

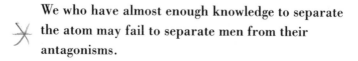

We who have almost enough knowledge to separate the atom may fail to separate men from their antagonisms.

XXXIII

The earth, to man, is an infected planet.

The human world wants to hear what is wrong
with it.

It is satisfied with the diagnosis.

It does not want to make effort attempting a
basic cure.

Man has a stubborn will to circulate poison.

XXXIV

The human fish is intricate and hidden; the appearances of his fins are deceptive.

According to what a man is called, so will people tend to respond to him.

Each of us has a so-called defect to which, in the eyes of our fellows and in our own eyes, we are reduced.

 To see the other person's defect causes him to see your defect. The result: you and he meet on the plane of defects only.

Thus we down-grade human experience.

XXXV

Races are real; but, to men, races are prejudices.

Nationalities are real; but, to men, nationalities
are prejudices.

Types are real; but, to men, types are prejudices.

The sexes are real; but, to men, the sexes are
prejudices.

Man is a prejudice to himself.

XXXVI

The human world is not yet born above the body.

Though our bodies are upright our spirits are still curled—or in chaos.

A child is a cosmos approaching adult chaos.

We can sense social form (a form superimposed over adult chaos); we have little or no ability to sense psychological form.

Our form is a malform, the form of chaos. Our organization is external. Inner unity, if it does exist, exists only as effort.

XXXVII

A teacher is one who brings tools and enables us to use them.

Practical intelligence is that which relates need, means, and object.

We cannot be given understanding. We can be rightly presented with proper material for understanding.

In this multiple simultaneous world words only dole out one thing at a time.

One may receive the information but miss the teaching.

XXXVIII

At best, education is a means of acquiring other people's ideas and habits.

At worst, it is a system of misfortunes. It is a systematic imposition of abnormalities upon normal being.

Each wrong idea kills one right instinct.

His knowledge may be your superstition.

Intelligence always is a voluntary contribution.

XXXIX

Let your own case prove the ignorance of others.

Be skeptical of everything save your capacity to make a fool of yourself.

No stupidity is so gross but what it finds some person willing to commit it.

Some stupidities are more amusing than most sense.

It is only half bad to be absurd in the face of the ridiculous. It is shameful to be ridiculous in the face of the significant.

XL

Each of us has in himself a fool who says I'm wise.

Most novices picture themselves as masters—and are content with the picture. This is why there are so few masters.

 When I speak I am persuaded.

People mistake their limitations for high standards.

Ordinarily, each person is a cartoon of himself.

XLI

When he uses his mind he is intelligent; when his theories use his mind he is stupid.

It is easier to think for others than for oneself.

Your mind is quick in following itself, slow in following mine.

He who cannot imitate must remain a fool. But he who imitates may become either a monkey or a master.

Aim to use insanity as a means of developing reason.

XLII

Too often the mind goes on what should be a
voyage of discovery only to return with no more
than it started with.

To understand a new idea break an old habit.

Only the plastic person can experience, for only he
is able to form and to take forms.

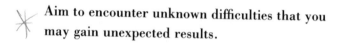 Aim to encounter unknown difficulties that you
may gain unexpected results.

By exhausting your ordinary surface force you
will be compelled to learn to use your magical
deep force.

XLIII

It is only in conditions of fruitful stress and suffering that our real forces become active.

Without tensions a person is nothing. With tensions, he is strong just in proportion as they are strong, he is significant just in proportion as they are significant.

Few people experience true tensions, true oppositions.

We experience conflicts; what could and should be tension, what should be opposition, usually degenerates into conflicts.

A conflict wastes energy; a tension generates it.

XLIV

An artist is he who can balance strong contrasts, who can combine opposing forms and forces in significant unity.

Real art demands the intense purity and wholeness of the very materials we artists often irresponsibly mutilate.

One must become a man before he can be an artist.

Far above a single talent I prize a multiformed man.

Art is a means of communicating high-rate vibrations.

XLV

Human society is organized not at the level of force but at the level of inertia.

In activity we go to sleep standing up. In leisure we go to sleep lying down.

Activity has become the mere accompaniment of over-production and over-consumption.

We move and hustle but lack rhythm. We have a sense of moving about; we have no sense of rhythm.

The world spins slow when it is empty. The slower it spins the more we cry for speed.

XLVI

While the world produced by science, the technical industrial world, is growing more materialistic, science itself is growing more immaterial.

Fatalism in the East is expressed. In the West it is comparatively unexpressed.

But it is experienced by the people of both regions, for the basic conditions of life are similar in both.

The West no less than the East feels bound by an unyielding yoke.

Morality is the determination not to be determined.

XLVII

While an increasing number of materialists are committing suicide because they believe they have no soul, an increasing number of spiritualists are going crazy because they believe they have one.

The existence of the body, like the existence of the soul, is a matter of belief.

The assumption of existence rests upon an uninterrupted and unchallenged series of pictures.

If all is belief, then wisdom consists in selecting the most fruitful belief.

We sleep: who profits by our dreams?

XLVIII

Science is a system of exact mysteries.

Materialists are hedonists who have not yet told themselves what they are living for.

This is a spiritual squid: a person groping towards "spiritual truth," no eyes, all feelers.

To domesticate an animal means to reduce its behavior so that it can do no more than a man.

The church fights the evil caused by a social scheme of which it is a main part.

XLIX

The candid Scientist: "We know there is something to know, but we don't know how to know it."

The candid Educator: "We know there is something to educate, but we don't know how to educate it."

The candid Physician: "We know there is something to cure, but we don't know how to cure it."

The candid Artist: "We know there is beauty, but we don't know how to capture it."

The candid Business Man: "We know there is something to sell. Watch us sell it!"

L

Walt Whitman's average man has turned out to be Babbitt.

Now that we have the term "racket" we can see how much business is business and how much business is racket.

The problem is not how to put life in business but how to put business in life.

The "full garage" means the empty person.

Democracy is the opportunity to skin anyone more stupid than oneself.

LI

Man is a breeding place of problems.

People are stupid not because they do a thing but because they repeat it.

Since I was stupid enough to get in this, then in it I must grow wise enough to get out.

We learn the rope of life by untying its knots.

"It" contains too much of life. I would reduce It to I.

LII

The strength of personality can be known by sensing how much it resists dying.

Unless a man dies consciously he will die.

There are eighteen hundred million living men. Living men must bury eighteen hundred million dead men.

More than one must go up or all will go down.

Man has no chance but the right one.

LIII

A running man cannot take a new direction.

This work is for those who are conscious of the need of a key to their own life.

"Man never sees himself."

Most needs are relative to bits of time; the need of consciousness is relative to all time.

To observe oneself is to conceive a new direction and a new being.

LIV

Men do not take impressions; impressions take men.

We are, it is said, creatures of impulse. We can become beings of form.

Being-effort is a self-activating force which needs no sanction save inner necessity.

I aim to form within myself a natural individual centre of functioning.

We must learn to bring into consciousness the meanings that have formed and ripened in our essence.

LV

Existence is in terms of long-distance objectives.

We must learn to use time as a curative agent.

A person's way of life can be modified; it is difficult to change his nature.

A man is not as much as he feels he is, but he is as much as he feels.

We do not have states of being; we have states of dreaming.

LVI

We should have right senses and instincts as to our functions in life. Our bodies should have sensibility.

We should be capable of polarizing corresponding beings, and of being polarized by them.

We should have feeling. We should have taste, and the ability to discriminate. We should have intelligence.

We should have a standard of excellence, values, and a real purpose.

We should have a living spirit and the ability to spiritualize experience.

LVII

Religion is that which relates one to oneself and to all other existences.

Participation depends upon similarity of vibrations.

Why am I, immersed in cosmic force, forceless?

My breathing is the Great Breath broken into nostrils.

If we have faith we wish to be able to prove or disprove by realization the faith we have.

LVIII

Man is a cross. The realization that man is a cross
is uniquely human.

We do not suffer: seldom does our essence suffer;
but pride, vanity, egotism suffer in us.

We are reluctant to accept the idea of having to
suffer impartially.

It is comparatively easy to suffer for everything
save normal being.

From a feeling of real helplessness there is born a
feeling of real helpfulness.

LIX

To realize responsibility is to realize with one's whole being that each individual is responsible, first, for the right process of his own existence, and, second, for the right processes of all surrounding existences.

True faith includes a feeling of certainty that man is basically normal; that, given right efforts and favorable conditions he can develop normally.

Doubt includes a feeling of certainty that man is basically abnormal.

Only those who cannot be inhuman will be human.

Disillusion is not a synonym for freedom.

LX

The objective is that which is. The subjective
is man's dream about nothing or about the
objective.

From dreams we talk to each other about reality.

Whatever is, is sacred.

The value of a thing must relate to what it does.
All things are real according to their functions.

We cannot begin to conceive of that Intelligence
which can understand and order a universe of
potentialities.

LXI

We who talk of knowledge of the universe cannot
sense the nature of an apple.

We assume that because we have the label we have
the understanding.

We are hypnotized by literacy.

A change of terms does not necessarily imply an
increased knowledge of reality.

There is a great difference between clear words
and clear understanding. Words are possessed by
everyone; few use them clearly; knowledge,
coupled with conscience, is life's highest prize.

LXII

Perceptions of reality are man's main food.

Each person at least once in his life rises to be a major critic of mankind.

The true critic is a critic of meanings and of values.

True ideas and true values grow strong in proportion as they are affirmed and realized by beings.

The science of life consists in deriving significance from all possibilities.

LXIII

There are only two things in the universe:
significance, and the possibility of
understanding it.

A partial recognition of futility is not enough to
destroy our conceit in what we habitually do.

The realization of ignorance is the first act of
knowing.

The realization of mechanicality is the first step
towards freedom.

The realization of nothingness is the first act
of being.

LXIV

The need is to find a method for developing essence and perfecting being.

This is one life: there must be one way of living.

If man were living as becomes him, then just this living, all life, would be the way.

We who are in the universe act as if we were not.

It is our task to suffer a conscious apprenticeship in the stupidities and abnormalities of mankind.